Complete Guide to Building an Information Security Program

Complete Guide to Building an Information Security Program

Connecting Policies, Procedures & IT Standards

David Rauschendorfer

Complete Guide to Building an Information Security Program; Connecting Policies, Procedures, & IT Standards

ISBN-13: 978-1-6872182-4-7
Ebook: 978-0-12345567-8-9

Cover design by Luisito C. Pangilinan

iRM
San Diego, California
United States

cybersecurityresource.com

About the Author

David Rauschendorfer is a former Marine who served his country leading military intelligence operations across both Iraq and Afghanistan. His leadership and critical thinking skills have driven him to his passion for protecting sensitive information throughout his cyber security career, making him a thought leader and true business partner.

As a business leader and information security consultant, David assists organizations in establishing and developing cyber security programs. With expertise in driving efficiencies throughout the organization's core business processes, reducing risk of exposure, and securing a brand's reputation in the marketplace, he reaches across business sectors to drive solutions that affect the bottom line. His thought leadership and business acumen place him at the pinnacle of his profession and have gained him the respect of his peers and colleagues.

Dedication

This book was written in dedication to the business leaders who maintain a never quit attitude in their diligence to protect their organization's sensitive information.

—David Rauschendorfer

Table of Contents

List of Figures

Preface

Every organization today faces an ever-changing set of threats in this digital landscape. Understanding how to develop a functional information security program to protect your organization's reputation and brand from being tarnished due to a breach of your company's sensitive information is more critical than ever. Developing a functional program that sets up the best information security practices across the organization's operational workflows is the leading practice for protecting against a possible breach.

Creating a set of policies that meet an organization's regulatory requirements will put a check in the box. This will not, however, lead to you securing your sensitive information from a breach. Understanding how to set up secured processes and a security-minded culture across your organization is the missing link to protecting an organization from one of its largest threats, its people.

Even if you do not have an in-house cybersecurity expert that can work to secure your Information Technology (IT) environment, you still have a responsibility for securing the sensitive information. This book will help you in creating a program that secures an organization's critical data and keeps its reputation intact.

Acknowledgment

A great thing about the information security industry is the many senior leaders willing to share their knowledge and expertise with those who are willing to learn. To those I have had the pleasure of working alongside, who shared their years of experience, I am forever grateful.

CYBERSECURITYRESOURCE

INTRODUCTION

Welcome to your guide in establishing an information security program for your organization. Throughout this book, you will learn the leading format for meeting your regulatory requirements by having a security program. But also, how to set up a security program that launches leading security practices across your key business workflows protecting your organization's most sensitive data.

In today's ever-changing threat landscape, you can't afford to only focus on setting up your information security documentation. Often, the human element to security is the greatest risk for any organization. You must focus on building a security-minded culture, where your documentation governs the way your core business processes function. This can be a daunting task without a strategic guide to follow using proven methodologies to help you.

By the end of this book, you will have the tools you need to set up your organization's information security program and begin shifting to a security-minded culture. Become the hero of the business by showing yourself as the solutions expert and be the business partner needed in your organization.

CHAPTER **1**

BUILDING AN INFORMATION SECURITY PROGRAM

Connecting Policies, Procedures, and IT Standards

The first thing you need to understand is how policies, procedures, and IT standards work together to drive your information security program. Organizations should have these three layers of documentation for their information security program to appropriately drive security practices. Outlining these three layers of information security documentation ensures that the program will be effective in driving the business's day-to-day operations, building security practices from the ground up, and protecting the organizational assets, reputation, and sensitive data.

Figure 1: Documentation Pyramid

Your organizational policies are the high-level statements that cannot be undermined without formal approval and will set the parameters for guiding an organization's security processes. These policies will follow a specific framework which the organizational leadership decides to align with when setting up a security program. They are very straightforward and to the point and should not be written in long paragraphs. They should be written in layman's terms, thus easily understandable to anyone no matter their information technology experience. These policies will be what the management team defines and moves forward within setting up a security-minded posture or culture across the organization.

Though this document may be several pages long, as you work through the security framework and address all the control categories and subcategories defined in it, do not worry that it will be too much for the average user to understand or put into practice. There is a reason why there is more than one layer of documentation, and you can aid each department in understanding how the organizational policies apply to their specific departmental processes. Often, not all policies will apply to each department, so as you move forward, you will need to define what the employee's role is within their department's information security program and how it ties to this policy.

Next, you will work on developing your IT standards and guidelines. These guidelines define the baseline requirements for all organizational assets. These standards will govern things such as your laptops, desktops, servers, applications, and databases you will be using, and the overarching network infrastructure and architectural setup used across them. While these IT standards and guidelines are often left for later when initially setting up the organization's information security program, they are vital in establishing proper governance and oversight of the risk exposure that the organization is comfortable in accepting.

Your procedural documentation for departmental information security practices is the official document that will outline the objective of the operational processes. This process document will be customized for each of the independent departments or business units across the organization. This may include departments such as Human Resources, Accounting, or other operational departments, depending on what your business case is. These procedural documents will outline the security roles for each resource within every department.

Each department may have unique use cases and business requirements where those procedures may go beyond what the policy considers appropriate. When this occurs, you need to document that the department has an exception and it operates against the policy. It is not necessary to change your policies whenever there is an exception. The organization's management team and risk acceptance authority should be made aware of these exceptions. Sign-offs must be provided by the proper risk acceptance authority and indicates:

1. acknowledgment of the department's need to operate against the policy, and
2. acceptance or provision of policy exception that will allow the department to continue using those processes or business solution

Connecting these three layers together to set up your information security program is key. Each layer plays a strategic part in driving security practices throughout the organization's operational processes. These layers also build off each other, so establishing policies without defining your IT standards will create a significant gap in your security practices. Remember, your IT standards outline the baseline security requirements that will govern your information assets. Establishing your security policy creates your set of rules, while then adding your processes and standards documentation puts those rules into action as they come to life within the day-to-day operations.

Understanding Organizational Culture

It is key to understand what your current organizational culture looks like and what drives the heart of the business's operations. Shifting organizational culture from wherever it may be today towards a more security-minded culture is a journey and will not happen overnight. Trying to implement security throughout the organization in a way that is fun and upbeat while driving an underlying security mindset is key to transitioning the current culture or further incentivizing security as a culture. Developing any culture throughout an organization is not a one-person job and needs the support of key leaders as they will be foot soldiers driving the message across their varying departments.

When setting up the organization's security culture, a key component is the leadership's perspective. Their understanding of security and the role they play in creating a security-minded culture needs to be confirmed and discussed. It is their leadership and management styles through communication that is going to drive the culture of the organization. If they present a tone that security is a hassle to deal with or something they're not concerned about, it will be seen as a hindrance. If this is your present circumstance, you are going to be fighting an uphill battle in developing a security-minded culture.

Everyone across the organization has a role in information security. Protecting the organization's sensitive information includes protecting the brand and the reputation that the company has worked hard to establish. If your leadership presents a tone that security is a business partner and something that they require from every role, it will be viewed as working well within the business processes. The security team can often find ways to enhance the business, using common solutions with secure functionality to drive day-to-day operations. It will set up a tone across the organization that security is a true business partner, and is a must-have in day-to-day practices, and that everyone has a role in using secure processes within their specific roles.

One key component in building a culture with a security mindset is defining the employee's role within the security program. This can be done with multiple facets to ensure that their role and responsibilities are clearly defined and documented so that when new resources transition into the department, the same security mindset and practices can be used in training. This is essential when developing your departmental procedures that outline the day-to-day operational processes used by the department, and the security aspects involved. This allows for the opportunity to show the security role of the department and the individuals within it. This will document the security aspect on whether they own a security control or process, if they are responsible for it, if they are advised about it, or if they are just informed. This allows you to build an understanding across all your employees that they have an active role in building the security culture because they are directly responsible or have input on the various security controls they use in everyday operations.

Another important element to building a security-minded culture within your organization is understanding how present and visible your information security program is across the organization. For example, when you walk down the hallways of your organization, is there anything that drives the need for information security? This may be things such as putting up items on a bulletin board to list the latest security breaches within your industry or using posters and funny memes that draw people's attention but also make them think about how secure their daily practices are. Another way you can drive a security-minded culture is by developing a newsletter, or if your organization already has a newsletter, setting up a security corner within it.

Implementing only one facet of these in your security program is a step in the right direction but will not be enough to ensure a shift towards a security-minded culture. The culture within an organization is rarely thought about or discussed, which presents an opportunity to gain bearings among leadership. The security team is where discussions about the culture of an organization can be openly discussed when found as a requirement for the success of the security program. Remember, your journey to shifting towards a more security-conscious culture is a marathon and not a 100m dash; it will take time and the proper steps to get to the finish line. Take pride in the small victories as staff start to ask more questions and bring to your attention small matters that they believe have security repercussions.

Meeting Governance Requirements

There are three main components that we are going to discuss concerning meeting governance requirements. Each part is necessary to build a strong information security program. Depending on the size of your organization and how your organization is currently structured, there could be a drastic variance in how these components are set up. The three components to focus on are namely, (1) organizational hierarchy, (2) information security officer role, and (3) establishment of an IT steering committee. Each part is critical for driving success. However, the order is not representative of the level of importance.

The first part to understand is your organizational hierarchy. There are so many different sizes of organizations that a single hierarchy outlining where security fits in cannot define success. If I tried to provide you with a specific example or outline a detailed hierarchy that I think would best suit an information security officer or team, it might not fit your needs as the hierarchy depends on size, budget, and operations of the business. No matter the size or the hierarchy that your organization has in place today, it is important that the information security officer directly connects to the leadership of the organization. If you work within a very small organization, this may be one and the same, and you may also be the CEO. For larger organizations, there may be a very complex hierarchy, so it is important that the information security officer directly reports to a

C-suite executive such as a CIO or CTO. Organizations have tried to place this role under the IT Department without a connection to leadership which has been detrimental to the security program. For your information security program to be effective in driving a security-minded culture, your information security officer, including his duties and responsibilities, need to have C-suite oversight and approval.

The second concept to meeting governance requirements is ensuring that your organization has an individual who holds the role and responsibility of an information security officer. Depending on the size of your organization, your budget, and your daily operations, this role may not be a full-time position. If so, then an individual within the organization filling other roles should still be named as the information security officer for the organization. This role needs to be clearly documented within this employee's job description, and the responsibilities should be outlined and communicated across the organization. This ensures that when a security incident occurs, the employees and staff know who to reach out to for their security concerns and who to report a potential breach of information to when a security breach has taken place.

The third most crucial part to meet governance requirements is setting up an IT Steering Committee. This committee is made up of department heads who will help in finding and implementing security controls that aid and manage their day-to-day workflows and departmental processes. To have an effective information security program, it is key to have the organizational leadership buy into the requirements being implemented. This assists in driving a security-minded culture through the communication and management of the IT security controls. A great example of this is seen when an organization decides on a standard for implementing automatic log-off functions to a defined length of time. It is common that many of the department heads and organizational leadership would rather never have to log on to their IT assets, being on their laptops or any other devices more than once a day. This is not practical for securing critical information, and an organizational policy should be established, driven by the IT steering committee's decision on what makes sense as an organization, not just at the department level.

Establishing Ongoing Maintenance

There is ongoing upkeep that needs the participation of leadership and department heads. These items should be discussed upfront and be provided with a level of responsibility for participation. Carrying out activities such as access reviews, developing departmental security procedures, and time commitments for ongoing IT Steering Committee meetings. All these activities assist in developing a security-minded culture while giving all levels of management a voice in IT management decisions.

As the leadership of the organization has obviously made a commitment to cybersecurity for the organization, they likely didn't know the commitment they were personally signing up for. Communicating leadership's role in security in a breakdown format outlining the commitments for review and signature of policy/process. Escalation of exceptions that are being requested which do not adhere to the policy. This can be documented and scheduled ahead with a context that senior leadership owns the responsibility for the security posture if a breach were to occur.

For the extended management team, if this is the first time you are asking them to take part in anything like a Steering Committee meeting or to discuss their departmental procedures, it may be a bit of a transition. It may take a few sessions before the committee gets into full swing. Outlining as much as possible before the first meeting setting expectations and talking points allows for a president to be set. Ask for others to share their points which may also be affecting the enterprise. A cohesive leadership staff will form from this group, finding more ways to solve problems and work together.

The core components of the governance structure allow you to communicate the importance of security and ensure that the current state of security is being discussed and presented at the right levels across the organization. Each part will help in driving the overall success of the information security program and ensure participation as it is communicated that everyone has a role in security. Find the best ways within your organizational structure to implement a governing role over security and stress the importance of the information and key performance indicators (KPI) that security presents as you work to reduce the risk of exposure to sensitive data as well as ensuring the brand and reputation stay in tack.

CHAPTER 2

ESTABLISHING ORGANIZATIONAL SECURITY POLICIES

Selecting a Framework

In this section, we will discuss how to set up your organizational security policies. The first key factor in setting up organizational-wide security policies is to ensure that you get the proper leadership buy-in from the organization's key management and leadership resources. These are the individuals that are going to ensure that security practices are being followed across the organization. They will also enforce these policies that are developed and communicated to every department.

When setting up your organization's information security policies, one of the first steps you must consider is understanding and selecting an information security framework. There are several frameworks to choose from, and there are often ones that are found and used commonly across different industries. The initial step in identifying what framework to use for your industry is understanding and defining your regulatory requirements. Based on the type of information you may be storing, processing, or transmitting through your organization's network, you will face different regulatory requirements. Some of the common examples are patient health information, payment card information, research data, or personally identifiable data. Based on the data types you may be working with, there are specific regulatory requirements and security controls that should be used to ensure the protection of this data.

You are likely using a specific data type that is governed by regulatory requirements and a mandatory security framework. This doesn't necessarily mean that you are limited to only using that security framework for your entire organization. There are many security frameworks that supply more detailed explanations for implementing them than what is typically found within specific regulatory requirement frameworks which can be used to meet your regulatory requirements. These detailed implementation specifications become easier to align, too, as they supply more clarity and understanding of how to meet the objective of your regulatory requirements.

Many regulatory frameworks used in various industries are very broad, thus leaving a lot of room for questions. It is within these grey lines that an organization can find itself in trouble as they work to develop their own understanding of what the requirements are for the security controls that are set to be implemented. There are many other frameworks that can be used that supply more detail in the implementation specifications for specific control requirements, which can be easily mapped to your industry's regulatory requirements. Common mappings from various frameworks can be found, which creates a line from the regulation to how your selected frameworks meet the requirements. This limits the grey areas and the need to develop one's own guidelines based on individual expectations of the requirements and its specific regulatory purposes.

A common framework established within the healthcare industry is the NIST CSF framework, developed by the National Institutes of Standards and Technology. There are many other frameworks that can be used that are commonly seen in this industry. There is no right or wrong framework to use, though an organization needs to

Identify

Develop the organizational understanding to manage security risk to systems, assets, data, and capabilities.

The activities in the Identify Function are foundational for effective use of the Framework. Understanding the business context, the resources that support critical functions and the related security risks enables an organization to focus and prioritize its efforts, consistent with its risk management strategy and business needs.

Asset Management - Business Environment – Governance - Risk Assessment - Risk Management Strategy - Supply Chain Risk Management

Protect

Develop and implement the appropriate safeguards to ensure delivery of critical infrastructure services.

The Protect Function supports the ability to limit or contain the impact of a potential security event

Access Control - Awareness and Training - Data Security - Information Protection Processes and Procedures – Maintenance - Protective Technology

Detect

Develop and implement the appropriate activities to identify the occurrence of a security event.

The Detect Function enables timely discovery of security events.

Anomalies and Events - Security Continuous Monitoring - Detection Processes

Respond

Develop and implement the appropriate activities to take action regarding a detected security event.

The Respond Function supports the ability to contain the impact of a potential security event.

Response Planning – Communications – Analysis – Mitigation - Improvements

Recover

Develop and implement the appropriate activities to maintain plans for resilience and to restore any capabilities or services that were impaired due to a security event.

The Recover Function supports timely recovery to normal operations to reduce the impact from a security event.

Recovery Planning – Improvements - Communications

Figure 2: NIST CSF Framework

ensure they are meeting specific regulatory requirements as outlined and defined by the datasets. Another part to understand when selecting a security framework for developing your information security program is the cost factor. Much of the cost factor when setting up an information security program comes with the purchase of new infrastructure that is incorporated to better protect the confidentiality, availability, and integrity of the organization's data. There are some frameworks that can be implemented that require added costs with advantages depending on your organizational operations and the business drivers. Obtaining a security certification often depicts a level of trust and certainty that the solutions you are providing to your clients use the best security practices available.

Many organizations sell solutions to their clients and look to obtain a SOC II or HITRUST certification. These certifications, like many others, can be obtained for a specific solution, set of solutions, or across the entire enterprise. In most cases, because of the cost factor, organizations can certify specific solutions instead of certifying the entire organization, but these certifications often require annual renewal. There are benefits to becoming certified within one of these frameworks, but it is up to you to establish which certification best fits your needs and ensures you understand the cost requirements on an ongoing basis for the specific certification frameworks you intend to use.

Because these policies will drive the operations and must have leadership approval, they should bear the signature of a C-suite level individual in the organization. When these policies are initially set up, you will need to ensure that the proper leadership takes the time to review, understand and ask questions about any policies they may need further clarification on. In order for your information security policies to drive operational processes, they need to be understood throughout the organization by all levels of resources, and if questions arise about what a policy is, the organization's management team needs to be able to clarify it upfront.

Another crucial aspect for setting up your information security policies and ensuring you have the proper leadership buy-in is to define what it means to the organization when someone breaks a policy. These policies will secure not only the operational practices but also the organization's reputation. One way that leadership can set the tone of seriousness towards the organization's security operations is to set up a sanctions policy that defines the management of disciplinary actions that need to be followed when resources deliberately or unintentionally break organizational policies.

As you communicate your organizational policies and further drive a security-minded culture across your enterprise, there will be several instances where individuals will break organizational policies unintentionally. There must be an understanding of what punishment for breaking these policies are, but you do not want it to be such a harsh punishment that employees fear telling when something is against the policy. If the punishment does not fit the crime, your organizational resources will never inform you of broken policies.

In that same context, not every event or security incident needs to lead to termination. If significant events are not addressed, your program may not be as effective as you wish it to be due to a lack of a security-minded culture. When resources unintentionally break organizational policies, it often requires added training that the resource would have to complete to understand what the policy is, why it is in place for the organization, and how they can adhere to it.

Establishing your organizational security policies to develop a process and understand how you will manage exceptions to the security policy is another important element. Not every aspect of the organization may be able to adhere to the policies as it will create unnecessary stress and increase inefficiencies in operational processes. You should not be creating policies you believe will fit every process or department's needs. Your information security policies are there to show a foundation of what security practices should be followed across the entire enterprise.

As you work to document your information security processes across every department, you will be able to easily find what policies are not being adhered to within that department's day-to-day operations. These are what we would call exceptions to the rule, or exceptions to policy. These exceptions should go through a review and approval process which would require the organization's leadership to sign off on the department using these exceptions to policy. It's not saying that the department cannot use these processes; it is a means of creating oversight in reducing undue risk to the organization if a process is not needed or the risk can be mitigated in some way.

Establishing and effectively communicating these key components when ensuring the proper leadership buy-in for your information security program will greatly increase your effectiveness upon its implementation. These aspects will drive the ability to appropriately govern your program and all leadership to feel as though they have a more active role than they may have realized in overseeing information security. Do not downplay the importance of gaining leadership buy-in: it can make or break your success. Therefore, ensure you follow these notes to set up and implement your program.

Developing Policies

Now with your selected security framework, it is time to start developing your information security policies. Using the chosen framework, build the first outline of your policy document following the categories and subcategories of the chosen framework. Don't worry about filling in all the details currently. Right now, it's a formatting process and ensuring that you are covering all the relevant areas as defined by the framework. This will likely leave you with a lengthy document that you can then begin filling in the blanks for the security controls implemented later.

When writing the policies about the security controls in place, remember that these are our high-level statements defining required outputs of how the control will be used at the enterprise level. How each department incorporates these policies will be fully documented within each department's process documentation. You may need to work with certain departments, such as your IT and networking leads, in order to fill in subcategories and understand how the organization implements and manages certain security controls and requirements.

The goal is to work through the categories and subcategories defining what the policy statements are for each of the security controls. In the instance where there is no security control in place, the goal is to define what the organization wants to implement to meet that security requirement. Just because it is a security policy that gets signed off on and approved to put into action, that does not mean that the organization must meet every single policy defined within their operational processes.

Policies are the guidelines that set the right and left parameters that the organization wants to work with. If the legacy operations are not following these policies today, then a remediation plan or corrective action plan should be documented. Each security gap should be given a risk rating and managed through a risk register or other risk mitigation tracking system. Set a priority and a timeline for the organization to work on implementing security practices that align with the organization's approved policies.

Organizational Buy-in

With the core of the policy outlined and reviewed by the proper security and IT teams, it is time to get organizational buy-in. The management structure across the organization are the individuals who ensure policies are adhered to and look to bring the best security practices and culture within their departments. Allowing management staff to take part in developing the policy set ensures they understand the individual policies. This will allow you to gain critical feedback from across the organization on the policies initially outlined before they go through a formal approval that each department is expected to act on.

When working with the management teams across the organization, be sure to set the precedent that these policies are being defined to govern the whole organization. Individual exceptions per department will be managed separately, and mitigating controls will be documented within the departmental procedures. The intent is not to create a policy that allows less secure practices to occur to accommodate a single operational process used by one department. Rather, the policies will support the organization's security culture by using best practices wherever possible.

It may take several sessions in the managerial meetings for this policy set to be properly discussed and allow for proper buy-in and questions. Often when this is taking place, it is done through the IT Steering Committee or ongoing management meetings. Depending on the size of your organization, this may not be appropriate. Use proper judgment on how to best complete this task. If you are the only business leader and you are working with an outsourced IT Department, then it will be up to you to drive this activity and work with the IT Department to understand the best practices of what they have implemented.

Additional Policies

Your core information security policy will drive 95% of your business operations security practices, though there may be several other policies you may look to implement to further manage your operational environment outside of this core security policy. During the development of your first policy set, you may find that some of the areas within which you work are not covered by the framework you selected. Every business is unique and often has a few operational processes not fully covered by an information security framework. These added policies are items you would often require the signature of for the resources that would be using these processes.

A few examples of added policies would cover processes such as governing a remote workforce. This is where you are allowing individuals to work from home or remotely, and you need a policy to govern their access and integrity of data used within their processes. Some other items you may set apart from your core policy set are things such as an acceptable use policy. This will define the requirements a resource has to follow to use organizational equipment and network activity, which will govern things such as authorized websites and social media use. Another very common policy used and required in the healthcare industry is a sanctions policy. This policy highlights the actions taken against resources who do not follow the organizational policies as defined for them.

All the added policies I have outlined will often require a signature from the organizational resources to ensure that they have read and understood the intent of the information provided. Start to think of other operational processes that your organization might be using in their everyday practices that could be defined as security limitations but are not currently being governed by your core information security policy. Ensure you are implementing secure practices across all operational processes used throughout the enterprise.

CHAPTER **3**

IMPLEMENTING ORGANIZATIONAL SECURITY POLICIES

Communicating Policies

There are several ways you can communicate your information security policies to all staff members. One of the first introductions to your organizational policies would be when you bring in new resources for roles that your organization needs. These new hires often go through new hire training and can be introduced to the organizational policies during onboarding to the organization.

Every new employee should be trained on the overarching information security policies. Upon completing training, everyone should sign a statement verifying they received the organizational policies. This verification would ensure proper evidence of completion of security training for your staff. Knowing the role of the individual in the organization is critical to ensure that they are properly trained to protect sensitive data.

Though indoctrinating new resources into your organization is a critical aspect to ensure that they adopt the security culture. The proper mindset to drive security practices is not likely going to get memorized from all the policies on their first day. Allow for ongoing access to policies and communicate the location they are stored.

This will ensure that they can appropriately reference organizational policies at any time if there are questions.

Supply a point of contact to the proper security personnel for resources to ask questions. If and when they do not understand the context of the security policy as it pertains to their specific role. This ongoing access is often delivered through an internal intranet site or any other common communication methods already in use. Be cautious in creating new communication channels that are not commonly used in daily activities. They are often forgotten or never referenced when questions or updates occur. Persistent reminders and training are needed to obtain a level of understanding required to drive your security culture.

While resources integrate into their organizational role, it is important that they understand what role their position plays in the information security team. Everyone across the organization plays a role in protecting the organization's critical data and reputation, keeping the brand in strong standing within the community and industry sector. Department managers should be teaching their new resources security procedures while training them on their role-specific duties. This will become easier for them as you work with the different departments to develop their individual security processes and define their specific roles within them. If the department leaders or managers do not understand their role in security and what their responsibilities are based on the operations they perform for the business, it is the security professionals' job to supply clarity and guidance on the department's role in security.

Understanding their day-to-day responsibilities will help in creating specialized training for privileged users and their role in securing the organization's critical data types. There are some circumstances, depending on the roles in the organization, where specific resources may require more one-on-one training designed specifically for that role if they hold elevated privileges or administrator access over others within the organization. Often, these are the IT administrator roles or specific leadership roles that have elevated levels of access and administrative duties within the organization. Ensure these roles are documented as you work with the departments and understand who has what responsibilities over the security controls delivered to their department.

Tracking Acknowledgement of Policies

It is key to ensure that you track and document every resource's acknowledgment and participation in information security training. This should be done during new hire introductions to the organization, where you can introduce them to their role, the information security policies, and any added policies that may pertain to their role specifically or may require a signature. Ongoing training should be conducted and documented on an annual basis.

As a baseline, a sign-in sheet can document which resources have gone through training. Be sure to provide them with takeaways, such as a copy of the policies or training material discussed during that session. This would be very similar to introducing new resources to an employee handbook. It is possible that policies can be incorporated into the employee handbook depending on the size of the organization. Either way, you will be required in the event of an audit to prove that all organizational resources have completed training.

Though it is key to train all new resources, it is critical to ensure that ongoing training is conducted at a minimum annually. The annual training should use the same format of resource completion tracking so you can show who still needs training. Work with the management staff to ensure all resources have completed their annual training requirements. You cannot hold resources accountable for upholding and keeping organizational policies if they have not acknowledged receipt of these policies or can say they never received training. Documenting each resource's participation in annual training ensures that they understand the organizational requirements, how they pertain to their job, and their individual role in information security.

Delivering Training and Awareness

When it comes to delivering your information security training and awareness program, ensure that the regulatory requirements you face for tracking the acknowledgment of this training are understood. You will want to implement the best practices available to you for delivering these training sessions to your organization. Maybe your organization is already delivering some training, and sticking to a consistent format may receive less pushback than creating a new delivery method. Implementing a testing procedure, no matter how basic, will aid you in gauging the audience's level of understanding of the provided training.

There are many solutions that can help you in documenting and delivering your training and awareness program. Many of these solutions will provide you with an exact list of participants ensuring the thoroughness of your records in documenting who has completed the training in your organization. If creating a training and awareness program based on specific regulatory requirements is a very daunting and overwhelming task, there are also solutions that supply a prepackaged training series that can meet your organization's requirements. These solutions can supply training that is conducted thoroughly and accurately that will meet the requirements set forth by the regulations governing your organization. They can supply a full start-to-finish program or a custom-tailored solution based on your needs and budget types.

There are many ways an organization can deliver information security training and awareness while driving a security-minded culture. Outside of the standard new hire training and annual training program, other security measures and awareness insights can be supplied to keep security a top priority and drive a secure culture. Using security posters around the organization is a great way to keep up the presence of security. Other great factors that can be used would be adding to the organizational newsletter if one exists by implementing a security corner. Supplying industry insights into data breaches and security issues and impacts that face the industry you serve makes the need for security feel more real and relevant to your organization.

Another commonly fun way to keep security top of mind is by implementing a screen saver upon lockout of organizational assets. Using security memes and posters in a fun and lighthearted manner as a screen saver keeps resources thinking security. Using these methods is a great way to remind resources to stay alert and conscious of their impacts in driving secure processes within their department and individual roles. Finding fun and creative ways to add security-centric initiatives into the operational workflows allows you to build an army of security practitioners across the organization, no matter what their daily role may be.

Figure 3: Security Meme

The key to implementing your information security policies is to understand that at this step, there are not likely to be any big revelations within the culture and mindset. It is essential to have leadership support throughout the implementation phase. Resources need to understand that this initiative is completely supported, and not complying will call for consequences. How these resources understand these policies will be further instilled later in the development of their departmental procedures. Delivering these requirements upfront allows for them to be properly referenced later.

CHAPTER **4**

DELINEATING EMPLOYEE'S SECURITY RESPONSIBILITIES

Promoting Good Security Practices

It is important to promote a positive and security-minded culture throughout the organization. Your top-level management team are not the only ones responsible for creating the organization's culture. Everyone has a role in developing a security-minded culture throughout the organization as it applies to their specific departments and their roles. The security role they play can be found in their day-to-day operations, even if they don't recognize it today.

Everyone within the organization has a role in keeping the information and sensitive organizational data secure during daily operations. This includes promoting the security-minded culture as new resources join the organization. Making security a fun, lighthearted environment rather than a ruler with a big stick will keep individuals honest while promoting good security practices. You don't want everyone to be putting away sensitive data or only logging out of their computer when they walk away while you are standing next to them. Understand business needs to move forward and find how you can work together with the business.

Each department across the organization must hold each other accountable for practicing security-minded behaviors. Each department understands its specific role in the organization's operations and how its daily activities affect the organization. The security staff will not always be present to ensure practices are following the best security procedures. Having a solid security-minded culture not only protects the organization's reputation and brand within their industry but also promotes internally the understanding of why security is a process that needs to be followed.

As the culture matures and develops over time, security becomes a top priority, allowing for newly developed business processes to integrate into day-to-day practices naturally. This makes the security team's job much easier as they know that secure practices are being implemented within new solutions and business processes. Established guidelines for these processes leading to the development of a security-minded culture will continue to pay dividends year after year.

Identifying Security Events

Your organization's resources are the first line of defense against security breaches. Unnecessary exposure of critical data may lead to a security breach which can tarnish the organization's reputation. Not everyone is intentionally trying to cause harm or increase the risk of data exposure when they are requesting information. There is no harm in resources questioning someone's need to know, especially if it seems out of place and unnecessary for that person's position. Empowering the staff who manage the day-to-day practices to become security warriors will be a key element in finding success within your information security program.

Throughout your information security awareness and training programs, ensure you are supplying and identifying the most likely situations that can lead to a security event. This allows every department across the organization to become the eyes and ears of the security team. This ensures that the best security practices are being followed. When the best practices are not being followed, they can be found and corrected quickly.

When it comes to communicating and training the internal organization's staff which may include contractors, communicate the most common security events seen in your industry. A common way to share this information is by highlighting a few recent security events that have been reported in your industry. If possible, find security incidents that align with common business practices found across your organization. These breaches supply insights and can shed light on why certain business processes taking place today may be increasing risk of exposure.

Your organization has likely implemented high-level solutions to protect outsiders from accessing your critical information, though the largest threats are coming from your internal staff. Resources can make decisions that incidentally expose critical data to individuals who do not require access to the information to do their job. Just because somebody wants to know certain information does not mean they need to know it to perform their duties for the organization. Not everyone is intentionally trying to cause harm or increase the risk of data exposure when requesting information. There is no harm in questioning someone's needs to know if it seems out of place or unnecessary for that person's position. Another example is that at one point, it was common for someone to accidentally fax patient data to the wrong number, though this is not as common today.

Reporting Security Events

Every organization should have an internal resource named as the information security officer. Depending on the size of the organization, this person may hold multiple roles and duties across the enterprise. It is still essential to ensure that everyone in the organization knows who this named resource is. Even if it is not their only role, their job responsibilities should be outlined in this individual's job description. It should be communicated who handles security and how to notify them in the event of a potential security event as it is identified.

Ensure there is an open-door policy for anyone across the organization to openly discuss security concerns with the information security officer. You should be setting up a sanctions policy to allow individuals an understanding of what could happen if they break or do not follow best security practices as outlined by the organization. A security officer should not sanction those trying to do the right thing. After further review of a security event, you may find that resources are trying to do the right thing while still focusing on completing their tasks at hand. In these instances, continued information security training is usually the best course of action. These identified individuals who are not following the organization's security policies are not always acting with ill intention.

Since you now understand that internal staff and any individuals working with your organization are your first line of defense in finding security events. It is crucial to ensure that clear communication channels are set up and are easily accessible to everyone. As security events are found or if someone feels that something is not right with how their peers are completing their job, they need to know how to report this possible security breach. For resources to feel comfortable reporting events to the proper parties, they need to be able to do so without fear of retaliation. Allowing for anonymous submission of potential security events is a possible solution to ensure there is no fear of retribution.

Once security events are found and communicated to the security officer or the proper staff members, it is essential that actions are taken in a prompt and calculated manner. Because there are so many potential outcomes and scenarios that take place, we cannot go over every scenario and discuss the proper action(s) to take during those instances. Every event should be analyzed to understand its severity and threat of undue risk possibly placed on the organization. Not every security event will need to be labeled as a security incident, just as not every security incident will need to be identified as an information security breach. Understanding and developing the organizational guidelines and escalation authorities for each stage of incident management is critical in ensuring that events, incidents, and breaches are managed appropriately based on their severity and likelihood of impact.

Building a Business Partnership

Often, you will be seen as the solutions expert for the organization or, depending on the size of the organization, the business analyst. Aid the departments in finding solutions and efficiencies that help them in their day-to-day processes. As you continue to work through the documentation of each department's processes, you will likely have the greatest insight into the solution sets being used across the organization. These solutions may be able to manage different business functions and enhance multiple departmental workflows. Sharing this knowledge can enhance the relationship between security and the business. This may also directly affect the bottom line, thus making the security team and yourself key business leaders and newfound assets for the organization.

It is much better to be seen as the hero than it is the villain. Position security as the business partner rather than the one who holds everyone to the policy and is a punisher. There are many organizations that have many slanderous terms they call their security officials. This is because that is where the staff see this person, only when someone breaks policy and needs more training or reprimanded. Changing this perception and becoming a business partner with each department will lead to resources being more open and candid with the true state of security. Be the partner willing to help them solve daily problems and be on their side: it becomes much easier to streamline the culture shift when this can take place.

Finding the best role or position to play for your role can sometimes take time. Understand the current culture within your organization and see how that compares to where you would like to see it. Generate an action plan with steps you can take to start transitioning your role into a new perception if that is what is needed. Whatever your steps call for, the key is to take action every day and remain consistent in reaching the goal. The role you are asking your organization to play within security can only be successful upon your proper positioning of the information security program.

CHAPTER **5**

DEVELOPING ORGANIZATIONAL SECURITY PROCEDURES

Defining Roles by Controls Matrix

When looking to develop your organizational security procedures, there are several things that should be set up before diving straight into documenting individual procedures. Many of your organization's processes may vary based on the individual departments or within unique roles the resources may play within the organization. Often these varying operational functions are easily found through the strategic separations of business units or departments that can be found across the enterprise. These departments can be used as the common logical separators between security controls that will be documented within formal procedures outlining the organization's operational activities.

As you identify the different departments across the organization, you also need to understand who holds the responsibility and decision-making authority over the underlying security controls used. One way to document and show this authority is by developing a RACI chart. Once filled in, this chart will help in defining which departments across the organization are responsible for each security control used by the business. Often, you will place the departments across the top of the chart, which will highlight the various security controls initially found through the security framework used within your policy. List any other controls unique to your organization's operations on the left side of the chart.

Using a RACI chart is a very common project management practice. Developing this understanding of the security controls used and who has what authority over them is critical when developing your organizational security procedures. This chart will clearly show who is responsible, accountable, consulted with, and informed of each security control used. When working with the individual departments to further develop their operational procedures, it is key that they understand their role and responsibilities as it aligns with the chart. This can also be used to ensure that the departments understand that they are not directly responsible for many of the security controls they use day-to-day. Their input on how it affects their day-to-day roles is key in further aiding them in finding solutions to drive operational efficiencies within their processes.

Control Description	Responsible Individual	New System	HR	ED EHR Mgmt	PACS Mgmt	LAB Mgmt	Pharma Mgmt	Finance Mgmt	Facilities	IT Mgmt	IT Infra	IT Security	IT Service Dsk	IT Ops	IT Controls	IT Development	Steering Committee	IT Qual. Assurance
0) Information Security Program Management																		
0.a' – Information Security Management Program																		
1) Access Control			X	X	X	X	X	X				X						
Business Requirement for Access Control			X	X	X	X	X	X			X					X		
01.a* – Access Control Policy												X						
Authorized Access to Information Systems												X						
01.b* – User Registration			X	X	X	X	X	X				X						
01.c – Privilege Management																		
01.d* – User Password Management																		
01.e – Review of User Access Rights			X									X						
User Responsibilities			X									X						
01.f* – Password Use			X									X						
01.g – Unattended User Equipment			X									X						
01.h* – Clear Desk and Clear Screen Policy																		

Figure 4: RACI Chart Example

Outlining Departmental Procedures

With a solid understanding of who's responsible for the varying security controls used across the organization, you can now move forward in outlining your departmental procedures. The first step, much like when you were developing your initial security policy, is to start by creating a foundational template following the organizational security framework that has been approved to be used to drive your security practices. Utilizing the security categories and subcategories found within your selected framework, build the first template of how your departmental procedures will work, look, and function. Your first base template, along with your RACI chart, will be used to show the several categories or subcategories that do not apply and will not require documentation for various departments based on their operational duties and processes.

Each department's procedural documentation will be unique based on their individual workflows and business outputs. Not every security control that is used across the organization may exist in every department. Before you start having meetings with an individual department head to document procedures, you will first outline their responsibility around the security controls represented in the RACI chart. This will allow for customizations to the procedural outline to match what controls will need to be referenced within that department's procedures.

It is important that the department understands its role over the security controls used by the organization. Leading conversations off with reviewing this through the RACI chart can allow for a more team-spirited conversation around how the department functions. As you talk about the security controls, it may take a moment for resources to remember where they may be using that within their work functions. Offering more examples of how it is used across the business may offer new insights into processes that are taking place.

Establishing a Development Strategy

It is best to start with your own department and work through the process of developing your procedural document so you can find an effective workflow that can be used in further setting up department procedures across the entire enterprise. This will be a very large task depending on the size of your organization and the number of departments you are overseeing. After the initial setup, the ongoing maintenance of keeping these security procedures up to date is not nearly as cumbersome. You will be amazed at what you will discover about your organization and how the departments are managing day-to-day operations which influence your security controls.

After developing the procedural documentation for your IT security group, you will have a baseline to build from. The other departments can scale to their individual requirements. As you work to document procedures for every department, verify that you are using your RACI chart. Ensuring that you are not documenting security controls that the department has no authority in. As an example, every department may be using some level of encryption with their organizational assets and equipment, but this does not mean that they have any level of authority or management over the encryption standards.

Focus on all the processes the departments are following to complete their day-to-day functions. Limit the documentation so that it does not include organizational-wide security controls. It is often best to develop these processes with the various IT departments, who likely maintain the authority over the security controls used at the enterprise level. If nothing else, it provides you the context necessary to appropriately speak with the varying department heads about these security controls as you work with them to complete their procedural documentation. Work with each department documenting their procedures and help them in understanding their role in security as it aligns with their job functions.

Documenting Exceptions

While documenting the varying departmental procedures across the organization, you'll undoubtedly find certain processes that do not align with organizational policy. Understanding the need for these processes to exist is key to communicating why the policy exists. Understanding if something can be changed within the process while allowing them to adhere to the organizational policy. If the process cannot be changed, an exception to policy can be created. These processes will be easily named as you work with the varying departments on their core functions and how they complete their tasks required by the business.

When working with exceptions, understand that not every process can change to work with a format that complies with active organizational policies. Do not try and force every square peg through a round hole; all businesses are unique and require certain types of exceptions. Trying to completely change a process which creates inefficiencies in the business will not be appropriate. You must be willing to make exceptions for processes that must exist for the sake of the business. When these exceptions to the policies are found, look to understand and implement any mitigating controls that will reduce the risk to the business. Your job at this point is to document this procedure as it is today, make a note, and highlight that this is an exception to a policy that will be reviewed by management.

For exceptions to policies, ensure they are approved by the proper risk acceptance authority. Your organization may even document a risk acceptance policy that outlines which individuals within the organization have the authority to approve certain levels of risk. These risks are often found when implementing operational processes or solutions. Your business leaders will understand that day-to-day operations need to take place in the most effective manner possible. They will look to you to understand how, as an organization, you can reduce the risk of a potential breach but still allow the business to function the way it needs to deliver its outputs effectively.

CHAPTER **6**

ESTABLISHING IT STANDARDS AND GUIDELINES

Understanding Standards and Guidelines

Your IT standards are your formal requirements for managing your technical solutions. These standards set up a foundation for new solutions that are brought into your organization to aid with business processes. They ensure that new solutions meet your organizational requirements as they work to store, process, or send your organizational data through the best security measures possible. These standards ensure that everyone across the different departments, whether related to business initiatives or implementation-specific solutions, are all following the same protocols to ensure standard security practices are being met.

Your IT guidelines are the general recommendations that supply structure for following standards. These guidelines are often used when covering certain processes that do not require more formal documentation. For example, if your essential systems go down and become non-operational due to some unknown event, specific recovery processes to bring them back online may need to be set up. Systems may need to be restored in a specific order to ensure databases do not crash or based on the business requirements for the urgency of operations. This guideline can be presented in the form of a checklist to ensure that the IT staff performing the recovery processes understand the guidelines as they work to bring everything back online.

These IT standards will be used with configuration management for all new solutions and assets used by the business. Therefore, new solutions need to be configured to the security standards as they get implemented into your network environment. This will include managing configurations for third-party solutions being implemented to better enhance your business processes or work functions. These configurations should allow for the desired functionality required by the business once they are installed while ensuring the security standards are upheld.

If it is found that there are issues such as extensive updating, change requests, or added functionality, which was introduced by enforcing the IT standards, it may be time to review your IT standards and guideline documentation. Ensure you are still using the best practices with the current technology. Gaps may be found over time which may bring the need for further network enhancements as the business requires.

Structuring the Five Layers

The next aspect that we will look at is how to structure your IT standards documentation, more specifically, a secure configuration standard. Understanding the various types of assets and solutions used across the enterprise will help you to expand a core list of service layers. The standard list consists of five layers: desktops, servers, applications, database, and the network. Understanding, identifying, and documenting the secure configuration standards and guidelines for all these layers is essential in creating a secure infrastructure. Ensuring that the same standard is used to protect the organizational assets and the critical data used in its processes.

There are many components to understand and document when it comes to the configuration of these five layers. This standard will govern how the resources across the enterprise use and interact with the varying layers. The first set of configuration standards covers your configuration for access: how your resources will access organizational assets using their user ID, and the established privileges configured for their role, as well as the password configuration governing the requirements of using secure password standards. Next, you will need to cover the file configuration as it aligns with the various layers. Based on your data types, you will need to ensure a proper logging configuration and understand your requirements for logging each data point.

The other components can become more technical with your local firewall and required service configurations. Establishing standard antivirus configurations to protect those local area assets and their necessary processes. The remaining components cover documenting your requirements for backing up data based on the varying data types. The configuration for those backups and how they will be accessed, including the timing requirements for when they can be restored if necessary. Another configuration standard that must be addressed across the core layers is your encryption configuration, which may be driven by your regulatory requirements for your key data elements. And last is your network configuration, which ensures you are using best practices for segmenting your critical infrastructure. This ensures proper protection across the network segments, often using a demilitarized zone (DMZ).

A formatted template of a standards and guidelines document can be found on the CyberSecurityResource.com website. If you are working with a cybersecurity resource, your IT Standards should be provided in a format that makes it easy to understand and follow while customizing each layer to meet the organization's needs. It will likely take working with resources from different departments to fully document the requirements for each category. Ensuring all the right people are in the room will make the process go smoothly as conversations around each category take place.

Establishing the documentation for your IT standards and guidelines around these core layers and configuration standards ensures that all solutions and workflows are following the best practice. This ensures the organization is providing a secure environment through which your operational processes will function. It will set the baseline requirements for all new solution sets that get integrated into your organization for business purposes. Without having fully documented IT standards and guidelines, you are left with what the vendor solutions are supplying for security as they get introduced into your network. Not conducting any level of configuration, an off-the-shelf solution can drastically increase the risk of exposure to your critical information and could potentially lead to a breach.

Configuration Item	Desktop	Comments
4.1 General Configuration		
General: Inventory – All hardware and software must be identified and tracked using the LCM (Life Cycle Management) Inventory Management Process. Inventory agents must be installed on all servers and desktops. An Asset Inventory Sticker must be permanently attached to the equipment.	M	
General: Hardware – Hardware used for enterprise computing devices and end user workstations must be pre-approved by the IT Department, purchased through standard procurement processes, meet or exceed the design requirements, and be under an approved maintenance contract.	M	
General: Hardware, Minimum Needed – Only the hardware necessary for use should be installed. This could exclude the installation of hard drives, removable media (floppy and CD), modems, monitors or keyboards where not specifically required.	O	

Figure 5: IT Standards Example

Implementing Guidelines

As you work to implement your guidelines across the organization, think through the system development life cycle and ensure you're following a full life cycle approach. This includes the integration of new products and solutions, which will bring them up to par with your IT standards and reduce the long-term costs of retroactively upgrading those same solutions. Developing new solutions, either in-house or outsourced, must follow your organizational standards. As customizations are done with third-party solutions to meet your business requirements, these updates must also be reviewed, ensuring they meet minimum IT standards before they are used by the business.

Your production environment is where your active business processes are functioning. As you are supplying updates, patches, or further development work, ensure that only key staff has access, as required by their role, to that environment. This also applies to any ongoing maintenance that needs to happen to your solutions either internally or by your third-party vendors. These maintenance activities should be tested prior to moving into production to ensure that your critical processes will still function appropriately while keeping your secure standards intact. The last main part is the retirement of your assets and solutions. Ensure that systems are archiving and clearing sensitive data points in a secure manner and that you are following the best practice for the destruction or transition of these assets.

Work with your IT team to document the necessary standards and guidelines following the Cyber Security Resource templated download. This document may allow leadership some insight into what kind of work is being done, supplying some explanation as to why a standard was set. Some of the guidelines may be presented to the IT Steering Committee for review and approval. Several enterprise security standards may be too technical to bring to a leadership meeting and will be set with the individual who owns that IT process. Either way, work with the appropriate owners of each layer to properly document the standards and guidelines of each layer's critical control areas.

Managing Third-Party Solutions

In working with third-party solutions, it is essential to have a plan for managing the updates and patches or any other ongoing maintenance required by their solutions on your network. This is one of the most common ways that security incidents or breaches take place. It is often due to the unmonitored access of third parties you have created a data-sharing relationship with. These third parties do not need constant unmonitored access to your network. Always have a mechanism in place to monitor any third-party activity taking place on your network. Any configurations being pushed from third-party solutions with updates or ongoing maintenance should be reviewed to ensure that they still meet your IT security standards.

Many organizations are conducting due diligence against their third-party relationships and the solutions they provide upon integrating these solutions. But often, as the solutions are updated to add new functionality and flexibility within the data-sharing practices, no ongoing review is conducted. Ensure those third parties are still using the best security practices and meeting your baseline security requirements. As the functionality enhances, the workflows in the data-sharing relationship may change. Periodic reviews should be conducted to capture these new functionalities and workflows.

There is also a call for proper monitoring of the third-parties activity on your network. Also, the measurement of what has been delivered and if they are on target and in line with expectations. Understanding what the various third parties are doing and what level of access they have to sensitive data on your network is key. Ensuring proper security controls are implemented where necessary to limit access and protect against tampering of data. Engaging with various third parties is often vital in business, but those engagements should not go unmonitored or unmanaged.

CHAPTER **7**

IMPLEMENTING ORGANIZATIONAL SECURITY PROCEDURES

Defining Employees' Role in Security

Implementing organizational security procedures across your core business units is critical in driving a security-minded culture. This will use best practices and emphasizes the use of solutions to drive efficiencies across day-to-day processes. As you work with the individual departments in developing their information security procedures, an initial key component is using the RACI chart. This will be used in showing the responsibilities of the department and the processes and solutions used in their daily operations. There may be several occasions as you work through this process that you find certain solutions, applications, or business workflows that you were not aware of previously. Often, these processes have not been reviewed as they were implemented to ensure best security practices were followed, and now is a great opportunity to instill security principles into these workflows.

The key part of the initial setup is to document the responsibilities of the workflows used in managing the department's key data elements. There are likely several security aspects already being used by the department in their daily practices. Ensure that you highlight and reward them for using the security practices they have in place today. They likely did not recognize it previously, as it may be one small step in their overarching process. Rewarding the good practices they're already using emphasizes the security-minded culture already in place and reinforces the fact that security is not a hindrance.

As you document the workflows, align the management processes to those actively used security controls. Explain and supply a level of understanding of the department's responsibility for the controls they're using today. Ensure you communicate that you are not there to overburden the department's workload when discussing the security controls' operational processes. Using the RACI chart, show the departmental leadership what role they play in the oversite of the security controls they are using. Wherever possible, find solutions that the organization may already use across different business units, which may aid in driving efficiencies through other departments' business processes.

This is a great opportunity to further advance the relationship you have as a business leader with the individual departments. You are aiding them in creating process documentation that will aid them in their training of new hires and ensuring continuity amongst their team. This process should come off as very supportive and collaborative as you work across the departments to document the security controls that are in place within their operational processes. As a business partner, it is your job to make them understand their role in security and how they can support your initiative while showcasing the advantages that your information security program is going to have directly on the department.

Using Security Standards to Drive Informal Processes

As you are documenting the department's procedures, there will be several processes that are more informal in nature and don't need to be documented as a formal procedure. These workflows still need to align with your security standards, ensuring even informal processes are keeping the organization safe from a potential security event. Many non-technical resources may not fully understand the IT standards if you were to give them your formalized IT standards and guidelines documentation. You need to put it into context following the workflows and informal process that standard is being used in and communicate the security practices that they are already following. Look to find any situations where those informal processes should be updated to better align with the organizational IT standards.

You will find there are many informal processes known by a select few resources as they use them daily in their role and ongoing job functions. Identify the role that these informal processes play in your business continuity plans or disaster recovery plans. If something happens where those resources are no longer available to perform that function or duty, someone will need to step in to move things forward. In these cases, use a checklist or instruction guide to drive the informal processes. This will aid the organization in quickly reestablishing operational workflows in the event of a downtime occurrence. This process needs to be intuitive enough to be followed by resources who may not normally perform this function. These documents will supply guidance and understanding of what action steps should be followed by setting up an easy-to-use checklist for resources to follow and complete those tasks.

Again, ensure each department's procedure and the informal processes they follow day-to-day meet the organizational IT standards and guidelines. These standards need to be used as the baseline security requirements for all activity. This is your opportunity to explain the security standards as it applies to the department's job functions and their everyday workflows. Explaining why these standards are in place to protect critical data is crucial for ensuring these security practices are followed without your direct oversight. The checklists that align to your IT standards ensure these guidelines are followed when no formal procedure can be referenced, especially as new resources are brought into these roles.

Understanding the role of the checklists that are being used and their role will aid in the security teams answering questions if an incident takes place. Not all checklists have to be linked to business continuity requirements but can also be used by departments for standard activities used by multiple resources. If there is a standard process, implementing a checklist helps in eliminating deviations to that process which may reduce the risk of exposure of data due to having a basic checklist in place. Simple precautions are often the ones we never think of but have the greatest impact when it counts.

Identifying Solutions to Drive Operations

We've already discussed how you will be viewed as the solutions expert for your organization. This will naturally occur while you develop the departmental procedures and find different business processes that use similar workflows. Each workflow has the potential to be enhanced by solution sets already implemented by other departments. As the department explains their workflows and day-to-day processes, they only understand their needs and the requirements they are facing.

Businesses often become very siloed, with a narrow focus on their individual operational requirements. Often implementing assets and solutions with similar functionality to those found within other departmental workflows. Based on your industry, you will find many workflows used across different departments that produce similar outputs or have very similar capability requirements for the solution sets driving those workflows. Often, each department has gone out and bought its own set of solutions to meet these requirements. Creating an atmosphere of interoperability across the various business units will position you as a business leader and further you towards a position as the solutions expert.

As you work through the various departments and understand the many problems and solutions in place within the operational workflows they are performing, you can better understand the requirements of each department. Look to supply further guidance on solution sets that may meet the need of multiple business outputs. It is likely there are many solutions already used at the enterprise level by all business units. These would be approved solution sets from the organization's management where they have put out an initiative that the entire organization will use these varying solutions to drive business activity. If you can expand on this solution setlist and find opportunities to add approved solutions that will drive multiple workflows, you will greatly impact the organization's bottom line by reducing the number of third-party contracts with various solutions. This will streamline similar workflows while also reducing the risk of exposure by limiting data-sharing relationships and third-party connections to your network.

In every instance in which you can find a manual process and workflow that a solution set can further automate, you become a champion for that department. As the departments are explaining their processes, be sure that you put your business analysts hat on. Understand what they're doing to create the required outputs for each process, especially when communicating to you that it is a very manual and cumbersome process. Anytime that you can drive efficiencies and make life easier for the resources completing required outputs for the business, you will further enhance the relationship between security and the departments. This will help you reinforce the message that security is not a hindrance and is here to further support the business however possible.

CHAPTER **8**

MAINTAINING OPERATIONAL SECURITY PROGRAMS

Conducting Annual Security Reviews

With your information security policies and procedures implemented across the organization, the concern shifts to maintaining your security program and ensuring its ongoing relevance. Your security policies should be reviewed annually to ensure they cover your operational environment. As business changes and workstreams change, your policies need to be updated to reflect the environment. Ensure you are appropriately governing these new workflows across the organization. Any changes made to your organizational information security policies need to be reviewed by management which may involve an IT steering committee or another leadership council. Policies will make their way through a formal approval process, in which a final signing authority signs off on moving forward with implementing any changes. A revision history should be kept for all policy documentation outlining the date of the changes made and who made them.

Your departmental procedures should go through a similar annual review, but this shouldn't be nearly as cumbersome as the initial establishment of these procedures. Allow for an annual check-in and discussion around how any new security practices have been integrated into the business operations within the department. This should be a quick and painless process with each department. It will allow you to capture and understand any new workflows being conducted by departments. There should also be a point where any new solutions used by the department are highlighted to you. Ensure that proper secure configuration standards were implemented during the initialization of these solutions.

Your information security program annual review needs to be documented, outlining who conducted the review and any significant changes that came out of it. This will allow you to track the differentiators and verify that an annual review took place if an audit occurs. There may be times outside of the standard annual review time frame in which a significant operational change could deem it necessary to update security policies and procedures. Conducting this annual review will continue to allow the security team to gain insights into day-to-day practices and workflows being used by the business. This also allows the security team to stay aware of new solutions that have been implemented, and supplies the opportunity to further develop a working relationship between the security team and the business units.

Though these reviews are taking place on an annual basis, changes may be recognized throughout the life of the program. As you work through your daily operations, you will likely recognize the same questions coming up over and over or similar security gaps that keep arising. An information security program is a fluid mechanism that traverses the needs of the business and ingrains itself through the path of least resistance. The hills that will undoubtedly come up will require you to change trajectory to properly secure your every growing need and changing business environment.

Updating IT Standards and Guidelines

There are many situations where an organization needs to look at updating IT standards and guidelines as the business carries on throughout the year. Based on the solutions being used, there may be significant software updates that take place, which changes operational workflows for the business. As new versions of the software are implemented, ensure IT standards are upheld and remain relevant to the changing technologies. The organization should be tracking the life cycle for enterprise software to ensure that security patches and ongoing updates will remain available that uphold the security standards implemented at initiation.

It is well known that technology can move forward over a short time period. As technology changes and enhances, check that the solutions you're using are still implementing the best security practices with the available controls in that solution set. As new technologies are released, you may look to find cost-saving mechanisms where security controls have been enhanced to perform new functionalities, which may have required separate solution sets in the past. For example, as firewalls continue to be enhanced, integrating further intrusion detection systems has become less standard as the functionality has been updated within the firewalls to manage and govern these requirements.

Your IT department's procedural documentation may need to undergo more frequent reviews than other departments across the organization. Based on your RACI chart, it is likely that your IT department holds a lot of responsibility in supporting and operating several of the IT security controls. As they work to make infrastructure enhancements and upgrades, their IT security procedural documentation needs to be updated. The IT department will experience these types of significant changes more commonly since they're responsible for solution sets that affect the enterprise. These workflows will be updated more commonly than your standard business workflows and operational outputs used across the various departments.

Many organizations do not properly use their IT Standards and Guidelines or often do not have them documented at all. This causes inefficiencies when integrating new solutions into the organization where they may no longer meet the best standards that the organization should be following. If your organization works with segmented IT departments having this standard is critical to ensuring communication between each unit and that there are no questions on what the minimum requirements are. Without updated standards, how can the organization find when a solution does not follow the standard and needs to be granted an exception?

Developing a Security-Conscious Culture

As we have discussed throughout this book, a key part of building and maintaining your information security program is establishing the security-minded culture across the organization. This does not take place overnight, but with the right support from management setting the tone of the importance of security, along with ongoing training, the culture shift can take place. This will drive the security processes and build a security-minded culture. You need to ensure that you are keeping information security practices at the forefront for the resources across the organization. Finding creative ways to keep security present within the day-to-day operations is key to building your culture. Using security posters, fun, lighthearted screensavers, and a security corner in the organization's newsletter are all great starting points for keeping security a top priority within the daily work lives of your organization's resources.

Ongoing information security training is also an important element to use in aiding the ideology of the security-minded culture. This includes educating those resources who may misinterpret and unintentionally go against organizational policies. Supplying end-user training will reinforce the security mindset. Allowing for more opportunities for the staff to ask questions and gain an understanding of how it directly applies to them in their work lives. There may be specific roles or departments within your organization that may need unique end-user training. Based on their level of access and authority to your IT infrastructure and data sets, resources should be trained on their elevated privileges. As the security officer or security leader for your organization, you must reward and recognize those resources across the business that are doing the right thing and following best security practices in their day-to-day processes and departments.

To foster a security-minded community and culture, you must move away from an organization that views the security team as a hindrance, or an "us versus them" mentality. This belief leads the staff to believe that the security team is only out to tell them what they're doing wrong. There will be many times throughout building your information security process where management can highlight the importance of security and foster the team mentality of the different roles and business units across the organization. As security concerns come up, or common issues arise because of the security practices that the organization is implementing. Ensure that you bring leadership together and allow the different business units to have a voice in solving common security problems.

Developing and maintaining an information security program for your organization is not a one-and-done type of scenario. Ongoing efforts to ensure this program is used to drive security-minded processes throughout the organization's business operations are what will prove the effectiveness of this initiative. We have covered throughout this book the key components in strategically setting up and implementing an information security program for your organization. If you do not continue to care for this newly formed process, it will become old and stagnant and lose its intended effect. Ensure someone keeps responsibility for all the information security documentation with a directive of keeping it updated and appropriately communicated to all areas of your business, and you will find that the culture will shift in your favor. You will greatly reduce the risk of exposure of your organization's critical data.

References

Keller, N. (2019, June 10). Cybersecurity Framework. Retrieved from
https://www.nist.gov/cyberframework

Aamoth, D. (2014, August). First smartphone turns 20: Fun facts
about Simon. *Time*. Retrieved from
http://time.com/3137005/first-smartphone-ibm-simon/

www.ingramcontent.com/pod-product-compliance
Lightning Source LLC
Chambersburg PA
CBHW030954240526
45463CB00016B/2552

* 9 7 8 1 6 8 7 2 1 8 2 4 7 *